WORDS ARE THE WORST

Words *are the* Worst

Selected Poems

∼

ERIK LINDNER

TRANSLATED FROM THE DUTCH BY

FRANCIS R. JONES

THE POETRY IMPRINT AT VÉHICULE PRESS

This publication has been made possible with financial support from the Dutch Foundation for Literature.

N ederlands
N letterenfonds
dutch foundation
for literature

SIGNAL EDITIONS EDITOR: CARMINE STARNINO

Cover design by David Drummond
Photo of the author by Gerald Zörner (gezett.de)
Set in Minion and Filosofia by Simon Janson
Printed by Livres Rapido Books

Dépôt légal, Library and Archives Canada and the
Bibliothèque national du Québec, third trimester 2021.

LIBRARY AND ARCHIVES CANADA CATALOGUING IN PUBLICATION

Title: Words are the worst : selected poems / Erik Linder ;
translated from the Dutch by Francis R. Jones.
Other titles: Poems. Selections. English
Names: Linder, Erik, 1968- author. | Jones, Francis R., 1955-
translator.
Identifiers: Canadiana (print) 2021021760x | Canadiana (ebook)
20210217715 | ISBN 9781550655834
(softcover) | ISBN 9781550655902 (HTML)
Classification: LCC PT5882.22.153 A2 2021 | DDC 839.31/7—dc23

Published by Véhicule Press, Montréal, Québec, Canada
www.vehiculepress.com

Distribution in Canada by LitDistCo
www.litdistco.ca

Distributed in the U.S. by Independent Publishers Group
www.ipgbook.com

Printed in Canada on FSC certified paper.

CONTENTS

In "Island," an early Erik Lindner poem, "A woman is standing / at the window. / She's looking outside. / She's wondering / who's there." Questions follow: Why? Who? Often, in Lindner's poems, we know where: Seraing, Ostende, Duindorp, Lake Aa, Portbou, names unfamiliar and exotic to many North American ears.

The image of an attentive witness—solitary, patient, but filled with unease—bears itself out from Lindner's debut poetry collection into the latest of his remarkable poems, where we find "the eyes on the branches in the square." There's a notable consistency found in the six books of poems Lindner has published since 1996. They are replete with beaches, seas, wind, horizons and light. They are all frame, space, lines, and distance. They continually look. In "In Zeeland," the allusion to perspective drawing is explicit:

> A tractor drives at a snail's pace toward the dyke
> and as it moves eight lines appear
>
> and in the middle of each furrow behind the tractor
> stands a row of seedlings.

More often it is evident in the recurrence of waves, waterlines and sea shores where "everything hangs dead level" and "Light-lines on the horizon pull the sea into the sky." In the more urban setting of the poem "Seraing," set in a derelict factory, the horizon line dominates but shifts downward to accommodate the viewer's heightened perspective. A Lindner poem repeatedly places the external world in an existential relationship to a vanishing-point. Within this Brunelleschian grid, a duck swims, rowers move on the lake, a woman holds an umbrella, a child sleeps, a woman loses her umbrella, a "man is eating an apple in the park / and the trees bow down around him." This host of miniatures give us bearings on the wider reality engaged in each poem, drawing the reader into the frame like a Brueghel scene with its contrast of foreground bustle versus a skyline's boundless space.

Lindner's canvas of observation is scenic, but his palette employs neutral tones. The poems are consistently engrossing, vivid and haunting. They are also resistant to bombast or emotional outpourings. Nor is biography essential. No reader of Lindner's poems will find the name of his political party or his favourite ice cream flavour. His subjects express archetypes more than particulars and many moments of significance are often buried below the reported surface of the text. "The Tramontane" records a near-fatal diving accident but is written in such a way as to depict representative figures in a fable-like story. "18 September 1994," relates a visit to Portbou in southern France, where Walter Benjamin famously committed suicide while trying to escape the Nazis. What reads like a provincial seaside idyll is disrupted by the understated references to Israeli artist Dani Karavan's memorial to Benjamin, hinting at the deeper emotional and historical context.

Like many of Lindner's narratives, there's little exposition—even less so as his work matures—but earlier poems offer clues to the author's thinking. Lindner's descriptions gesture to abundance; they also express a longing for connection. "Tokens of identity" begins "What counts is that things should somehow make sense, / the chance to be part of a whole, belong to a group, / a collective..." The poem highlights a sense of separateness or exclusion where the lyric "I/eye" obsessively sees, but is at risk of not being seen, absent from participation. This central tension evokes a dilemma of presence, Sartrean in spirit: the condition of being absent from true being. Similarly, if we are "Witnesses at the threshold," we are at once permitted observation but denied entry. Beneath Lindner's understatement is the imaginative exercise of consciousness negotiating its freedoms within horizon and limit. The mundane becomes strange.

This duality is echoed in other sequences like "Wake" and "Rowers on Lake Aa," where the objective world is catalogued in order to comprehend and thus locate the fact of the self. The poems seem to be forming a relationship to their surroundings, half-way between affirmation and mystery. "This is what counts, the possibility beyond / the painting in the warehouse," Lindner writes. And if Ivens ("Ivens and the Wind") traps himself in a conditional state of inaction, agency is sought elsewhere in other poems with lines such as "when I walk toward the sea / I can go two ways" or "Water I need to see / so I can lose myself." In Lindner's coastlines and promenades, comprehension advances and recedes. The peripheral world promises clarity but provides no closure.

Lindner's obsession with vista, the eye and the act of witnessing are variations on a theme of consciousness, and the great benefit of having a "selected" for a poet as focussed as Lindner is to experience the writer's singular vision and sensibility as it accumulates over the course of several books. That sensibility emerged outside of Dutch poetic trends, sidestepping influences from earlier movements. Instead, Lindner's poems are wider in orientation, eager to independently engage on a European scale, where translations of his work in Italian, French and German have been enthusiastically received.

Words are the Worst, this first book in English of Lindner's poetry, offers to Canadian readers (and English speakers) a glimpse of his visual approach, where observations, via groupings and restatements, explore the nuance of perception. While the poems are direct and clear-sighted, their reserved commentary points at the elusiveness of written expression. Lindner's work seems pre-epiphanic to me, agitated from a silence just prior to revelation. This threshold constitutes a meeting-place between internal life and the world of things, an interim fertile with possible meaning, where "even a softly-spoken word / explodes in your ear."

David O'Meara

Words are the Worst

Couldn't find letter in the bin
and rattled about the difference
between what the reading wants to hear
and the intent that's somewhere else

and it feels so pleasant
it's so pleasant to see
and sounds so pleasant when there's a draught
but all aversions attract at first.

Caresses that ratify saying nothing.
Feigning haste, making your escape, and locking away the vehicle
round the corner, dawdling, spitting into the water.
The weight of time shattered by words.

It's time to give up speaking.
Give up the flashy rhetoric.
Give up disguising delay,
kicking out at the fleeting.

I can't stop you now.
You can't stop me now.
We're off to chop down a tree
with a nail file, knife and fork.

Island

A woman is standing
at the window.
She's looking outside.
She's wondering
who's there.

The boat to another land?
Service suspended. Still an island,
alone. She's stopped eating. Doesn't
drink. Sleeps in a white nightie.

On a platform under Mayakovsky's face
—who's promoting jeans, *keep them loose*—
we wait, as if we're thinking. Of a house.

With a woman
at the window
Her face pale
behind the unkempt hair.

Say thank-you, for chrissake, *please*
and always ask politely, politely.

I rang the bell, banged at the door
and called her name a few times.

Then there's a woman
standing at the window.
It's my mother.

She says: I'm your mother.
Don't think about it, all the bridges are burnt.

Reason

Don't start doubting how reason,
how reason, how reason, how reason.
A fly walks from the rim
to the middle of the tabletop
and back again, follows the edge
for a few inches, re-enters the void
of the off-white, tries again
I don't know what, and then flies away.

18 September 1994

1

All that came to be can disappear

How a long bench on a hot day
takes its shade from seven olive trees.
How your bottom feels clammy
at the touch of solid, age-old stone.

How the tramontane breaks the sea to waves
and with the piercing light of a sleepy sun
picks up the water's surface and swirls it
in hurricanes of yellow, blue, ocher, sand, water.

Fear of heights can dissolve, directionless.

Swallows which dive like bats along
the steep rock-face behind the bench
where the footpath snakes through three bays
but now points only to France.

2

Nothing chooses to die in Portbou

The girl from Aragon on the beach
takes off her skirt and strides antelope-like
through the surf while her leather bag
guards an iron-rimmed writing case.
She's here just for this Sunday
which is the same as a nameless history.

An empty socket on a steel baseplate.
The front yard of an abandoned customs post.
A boulder almost sliding into the sea.
Give it labels colour-blind there
play of tramontane, wind with all the force
of high mountains, sets you shivering in the sun.

3

All that came to be can disappear

Selling penicillin and morphine
over the counter. Inside the old guesthouse room
two beds stand between a wall of sickness.
You and I, who is masculine?

What is masculinity? The scrape
of a blade over the inflamed throat,
how it feels to be shaved
the last time, for a party

you won't be going to. Or the way
a child laughs and throws sand
at the sun. Falling and feeling ashamed
only when you get to your feet.

4

What never came to be can also disappear

Sand, roots, marram grass, footprints which
never passed here. The locals who stare after
the traveller but give no description.
Their goings still disrupted after a monument

was built. Now, as the tramontane licks at
your body and lifts you up, your spectacles too,
and bowls them along. Where the passageway leads
the churchyard to the abyss above the breakers.

Only the short-sighted can realise this.
How did it come here? Fifty years ago. For-
getting such things is barbaric. Even vandalising
an artwork is a sign of culture.

I did it. With no scruples. Today. Date.

Ourcq

As the icebreaker pulls away from the quayside
cracks craze through the sheet-ice,
from one bank to the other
the ship shivers and the ice buckles,
the surface heaves deep into the canal
and bulges and splits, crumbles and melts.

Now anyone can see
how heavy a swan must be.
The ice is as firm as its belly and webbed feet,
not white but transparent.
Where it stands
lies a layer of water.

Someone's scooping the ice from the fountain.
Someone's stacking tiles inside a crate.
Someone's raising the bridge.

The icebreaker comes nearer.
The swan keeps staring.

∼

If I'm lost for words,

or his voice that blocks them speaks out,
the child's hair is cut

before her tresses spread,

know then
that a hand

rarely pushes only to stop short.

Tokens of Identity

1

What counts is that things should somehow make sense,
the chance to be part of a whole, belong to a group,
a collective. People getting changed between
the low hedges by the barbed
wire round the dunes.

Playing-cards drop on an outspread towel, the picnic
under cloth in a wicker basket, sand heaped
over a bottle from the distillery where
one of us has worked that day. Like
everyone else we run to the sea

and back again, tap out the sand from our shoes on the path,
embrace what was left unsaid in every conversation
when we say goodbye and feel inconsolable
in a streetcar as the driver announces
the stops to his only passenger.

2

So brief, this sudden sense of bliss:
the Rhetoric Society's fool in the Leiden
Lakenhal with his dopey, gap-toothed grin,
the jester's hood and bells above his smock
and the shadow that the painter places him in.

To stand still and look at him
the way a portrait looks at you,
with no opinion, nor the slightest desire
to acknowledge where that laugh is leading
and to take up the shape which the space allows.

Pride turns to shame
with long exposure, still out
of place in a duffle-coat—waiting
on the museum stairs. Fool. The time
which is no longer in step with the other.

3

This is what counts, the possibility beyond
the painting in the warehouse—invisible
in the mirror of everyone's interest, his
eyes outlined as if with makeup: just behind

a handcart piled with mint and celery leaves
a market trader slowly tears the cloths
she's stretching taut across her belly, as naked
as if it hardly tips the scales, just a few ounces,

or a photo at most, a man walking and
seen from the back, an empty birdcage
in his right hand and the blur of the little
white dog running away from his sandals.

4

It's here, first illegal and then no longer
here still somewhere else in a crowded place.

You exist all the less and take note all the more
in the fact you're forever having to leave.

Someone starts humming as you pass by,
the impression persists, their look betrays them and yes

that's right, every time and that means never
once again you're just the other when you speak.

Stupidity's a luxury. Duindorp
final stop. End of the line.

5

Translate adultery
as adulthood.
You're a child.

It's all above
board, heavens, there's
nothing, we can do.

You blush a shade darker,
shadowy if need be,
which fits you well.

6

It's telling: seawall, raw fish,
Oranje Square, an empty bottle
left in the shower, the salt that wasn't
washed off. It's here. Look for it.

The mouth, opened into a question.
The turn in the wet towel takes
shape, needlessly and slowly
drags on and lets go—once again

the silent ride to the beach.

∾

There's blood in your lips
and yet the wind is whistling

and yet the metro is rumbling
underneath the table so
that your head falls
and even a softly-spoken word
explodes in your ear

your hair lies scattered
across the carpet
and yet your eye opens
and gauges in the light of the lamp
the dust quivering light in the air

and the fabric wafting down on you
too small for the table
too fine for the wind.

To Acedia

1

She is where she saw him.
(A sideways glance
at the oncoming traffic.)

The suitcase by his right foot.
A coat over his arm.

He asks: was her hand here?
He sits down on the upright case.

A hand burns on her belly
and a hand burns above
the car tire turning in the sun.

She wipes spittle from her lips.
Her fingers brush the sunlight off his suit.

2

Once a filter cigarette is wedged
into the slot of a matchbox on her knee,
she slides her hand into the V of her sweater.
Fingertips on her collarbone.

A pin on his suit. (Milk from the spotlight.)
Finely-striped socks. The edge of a thumb under a brooch.
A smile in a handkerchief moulded into a yawn.

Nothing escapes her.
No-one escapes her.

A tea-towel without a pattern.
A loaf without an oven.

3

It wouldn't be a proper boat trip without these birds
she says and on the guardrail
her hand covers the graffiti.

She has a skirt round her neck.
She's wearing yesterday's makeup.
A gust of wind frees her earlobe.

His mouth almost never tastes
of the cage in the hull.
Birds tap against the frame.

The Tramontane

The diver rests offshore in his story
to draw the cliff-face bare by the beach.
The wind shreds the story and frets and whets
the plane trees' leaves—the window-frame.

I came here with the wind for this story.
The path said a man ran over the mountain
and the story comes to a dead end at sea. The wind

lords it over his grave. And the diver gets caught
among the rocks, the helpers break the surface
and the wind smashes the breakers the sea.

The diver is painting squalls offshore. The cliff-face
is in bloom. And the grave is a step
that leads to the coral in a cave on the seabed
above the colour engraving of the floral curtain.

In Zeeland

A tractor drives at a snail's pace toward the dyke
and as it moves eight lines appear

and in the middle of each furrow behind the tractor
stands a row of seedlings.

The man on the tractor pulls the dyke toward him
pushes a lever forward and turns the steering wheel

to line the tractor up with the furrows just made
and starts a new route away from the dyke.

Six seasonal workers sit under canvas
on the back of the tractor two dole out the seedlings

and four shaded by the tarpaulin drop the plants
down holes in the bench in front of them.

Behind the tractor a pole is lowered with eight prongs
that ride along the ground the plants slide down them

and are woven into rows out of the workers' sight
looking at their hands they lift up the land.

Ostende

1

The bone lies in the sand
of an island that won't stay still

what's fixed is form
the history of wind
shoals of marlstone and rock

the wind is lost at sea
no wave has the same proportions

sand blushes red in the sun
on the racecourse where dust billows
and the hooves beat the same rhythms
the hooves beat the sand to smithereens

the wind runs across an island
where it works its former imprints
the marlstone of the beach
the racecourse by the shore
the rain in the sea.

2

The sea's as big as the wind
and flows across the marlstone
worked by the wind for the sea

a sandpiper runs along the wind
and counts with its steps
the free patches of sand
and the crests of sea blowing free
and the clumps of wind tumbling free

rolling creeping sliding pieces
of an island that briefly stands still
by the edge of the sea

hooves pound down the stone
the sea carries the bone ashore
the sand cools down in the wind

clumps of foam measure the outline
of an island emerging for a little while
under a sandpiper's footsteps

beyond the wind above the sea.

~

The garden lies between the road and the window
I saw through my dream by standing up in it

and still you shrug your shoulders
amidst what's embracing you

that cartwheel and that brick path
the chair which just stays put

how quietly streetcar seven to hoboken
circles round the tables outside café athene

one tree is lighter than the other
on the ground the sunlight falls on your feet.

~

A man is eating an apple in the park
and the trees bow down around him
the grass has run out of the treetrunks
it's jostling round his feet
the pond pushes plants to the bank
the man takes a bite of the apple
and lets it tip over on his tongue
sucks out the juice and crunches
the pond shrinks behind the shrubs
branches point upwards out of the trees
an animal climbs up a trunk
and leaps and sprints across the grass
along the green beside the street
back to the pond and past the shrubs
to a man who's folding his arms
on the grass in the distance in a park.

Back from Acedia

1

She knows how to wear a coat as a dress
while sitting she braces the tips of her shoes
against the floor

he stands he walks a few steps
he walks back and stands still again

she sees pin-sharp how straight the objects are
if she imagines the ground as slanting

reading in the bus as it sets off
she reaches out a hand
which a woman grasps to sit down

she ties her laces on the escalator
a car stops and she gets in.

2

As she puts her knee on the seat
she lifts the chair by its back
the chair balances on one leg
twists to a stop

in the stairwell stands a ladder

she says my thoughts are a landscape
her fingers drum against her thigh

a woman is squatting on a tree-stump
her elbows propped on her knees
no ankle on her feet

she stands up and opens the shutters
a man is dancing on crutches in the street.

3

After she starts the engine
drives a front wheel off the sidewalk
she rubs mascara across her eyelid

over the road a boy is spraying
a garden hose onto a moped
water runs in ripples across the street

a girl trying to skip
lands with feet outspread

a woman in a parking space
waves to the passing cars

she puts a map on the dashboard
she turns the mirror back and presses the gas pedal.

4

On Sunday she buys her little dog a croissant
and she walks down the corniche in a new dress
the shadow of the balustrade fills the sidewalk
the handrail curves with the sea's horizon as she bends down

a pair of sunglasses lies unfolded on a towel
a man with outstretched arms is throwing a child into the sea

the man who was speaking sign language
where the boardwalk widens out
clapped loudly all of a sudden
and even then she didn't stop reading

she swims and spreads her arms at every wave
up by the roadside a hitchhiker is sitting on a suitcase.

≈

The sea is purple at Piraeus.

A flag creeps out of the campanile
when the wind turns.

A man steps over a dog.
A woman stoops to rub her eyelid.

In an umbrella shop an umbrella falls off the counter.

A pigeon perching on a narrow branch
falls off, flutters, and settles again.
The berry out of reach at the end of the twig.
The branch that bends, the ruff that bulges as the pigeon shuffles along.

A girl gets on the metro with a desk drawer.

On the thick sand by the breakers
an angler slides his fishing rod out before him
a bike beside him on its kickstand.

He stands with legs apart as if he's peeing.
Birds' footprints in the sand.
The fishing rod arches over the sea.

≈

A stairway leads into the sea
a wave breaks across a step

a ship is pulling on its chains
bulging out its hull

a driver opens the door of the moving car
and spits the betelnut onto the receding ground

a rolling cigarette sprays a circle of sparks

leaves patter against the passing carriage
on the metro a man's still wearing his helmet

there's the rain putting out the fire

there's a dog guarding two sheep
and trotting up and down the field

walk down a stairway

push off from a step.

Klockmann

for Ruth

If there were a god then he'd have made you
polished your belly which he's blowing full of air
staunched your bleeding with mouth and bellows
and shackled it onto a belt or a chain
moved it to a cool place in the furnace

the knight is the only chess-piece with eyes
its mane sticks out like fishbones and fins
its muzzle strains toward the slot in the bishop's mitre
the king's cross the castle and pawn
the bead on the queen's hat

but god becomes grubbed-out hedges honeycomb gall
or anodised the dime the starfish
cakewalk at the fair the watermill wheel
almost under water an otter's whiskers
the jewels of someone in the bath and drying herself.

≈

A short woman holds an umbrella high above her head
you stop short to make a note and someone bumps into you

a woman loses her umbrella and chases after it
the umbrella tumbles across the street

as if the wind's the same as me

as if an umbrella's a boat on the pavement

a wall hacks out a chunk of sky
rain falls into your notebook

a girl asks you the way
if you tell her you'll lose her.

~

In the storm that just blew up
the road will soon be impassable

barriers go up after us
foglamps dim ahead of us

a little attic window on the left
level with the dyke

the figure sitting there
taps the table with a thimble

the child turns over in its sleep
the TV's playing without a sound

the corner of the fire escape
in the window behind them

she puts the newspaper in the basket
props her hands against the chair-back

counts the tiles as far as the mat
the cork strip along the doorjamb

sings beneath her breath
her fall is a hole in the snow.

≈

This forme fits somewhere
inside this house left clean and tidy
after the loft extension

the wardrobe its door a mirror
that falls on top of her
is held back by the tall chair
but she stays lying there
in the open triangle: floor mirror chair

did she pull the mirror toward her
and in it see the postcard on the ground

did she stack her clothes at the front of the wardrobe
shut the door
and see her reflection bending over herself
before her ankles gave way
and she fell to the floor

lying in a z she pleads
wooden wardrobe wooden chair.

~

When I walk toward the sea
I can go two ways

—ends of a line
traced by her index finger as she reads

a thumb and two fingers skim
as I walk toward the sea

the hillock in her palm
fingertips which pick up grains
rubbing them into the meat just browned

I need to keep it in hand
if it comes out of a jar
I can't feel it

she points which way to read
pricks the meat

when I walk toward the sea
I can go two ways
my fingers skim

I sift the sea.

Ivens and the Wind

Till the windmill's sail spins free
Ivens waits on a chair for the wind

till the peak of a dune-hill crumbles
on a chair waits Ivens for the wind

till the train dissolves in a plume of smoke
Ivens on a chair waits for the wind

till the dust brings tears to his eyes
on a chair Ivens waits for the wind

till the sweat on his chin dries out
Ivens waits for the wind on a chair

till the beards of the camels flutter
till the grains flit away like fleas

till a pennant's caught in a kite-string
till his walking stick swings like a golf-club

till the sand seethes like foam on breakers
till his suitcase lid flies open

on a chair on the hilltop Ivens points to where
the wind lies asleep in a cave in the desert.

～

I remember

The sea broke and all your hands could do
was turn into tools and scoop like mechanical diggers
each shovelful you tipped slid back on to your feet
no matter who mentioned a house a chimney a table
your nails kept scraping a flat floor in the sand.

I remember the ground shaking and how you stood there waving
with all those tattooed birds squawking on your arms
the lower the thunderclouds loomed the fiercer the waves
you schlepped handfuls of wet sand all the way up the beach
your elbows' wipers plastering the wall.

When the wind drops I know your birds will fall silent
the starfish you lugged home will softly fall off the wall
and I know how pale your legs stretching wide
I see the pieces of shell sticking up between your toes
all you can hide is your body in the sand.

Witnesses at the Threshold

1

Birds tilt at windmills
all in a whirl

barking by the houseboats
chains drag through the gravel

cartwheeling like clockwork
high in the sky

rainwater in a pool
on the roof of the truck

the light of the swaying lantern
over the row of doorbells

the gallery round the tower
its guardrail slanting outward

a river flowing
into a marshy field.

2

A plastic bag slides off a branch

and floats down onto the marketplace
where a girl is crouching to brush her hair
the key-fob clenched in her mouth
the teeth of the key pricking her chin

on the stage bouquets in a pail

two legs together, one
raised higher than the other

the black bird in the field
beside a tall dark tussock of grass

a shepherd resting his chin on his stick
as the flock jostles round him.

3

Horses teaching their foals to run
the horse trotting the foal cantering
the horse walking the foal trotting
past the tape in front of the fence
into the corner of the paddock

the dragonfly hovering over the water

rain splashes up from the paving
the garden hose chicanes through the grass

a bird hops onto the edge of a garden tub
above the bricks laid in arcs

sunlight traces a line down the corridor
and casts a windowpane onto the wall

the sprinkler sprays across a treetrunk
the mower snags against its cable.

4

Witnesses at the threshold we are
the candle burning in broad daylight
the orange lying under the bulge in the window

the sorcerer's apprentice holds out a hand
for his bride, the motionless cape, chandelier,
the green dagging on her sleeves

faithful as the dog guarding them
the brush on the chairback
the broom against the seat

we are witnesses at the threshold
no-one can hear them
yet somehow it still gets through.

Acedia

In the ground-down morning the plain's not empty
no tree is in blossom no field is sown
the earth is nowhere ridged or yellow

in the tattered half-dark the ditch is not dry
on its barren streambed floats the ghost of a man
his hand under roots tangled in sand

the morning star burns sharp through the mist
and stabs its barbs along the hill
and rips the land open as far as the horizon.

from Wake

Burning—borders of the clouds
sailing—seagulls as the wind rises

surfers on their bellies like the drowned

how waves slide along the breakwater
how their peaks jut forward

how foam on the sand flutters in the wind
and breaks free and rolls further

how the foam washing ashore pushes the backsliding foam
further on

how a wave breaks
and only then makes foam

how the white foam of a new wave
slides like a tongue through brown dried foam

how the seawater swirls
and slaps against the pier

wave-crests overtopping the breakwater
rain leaping out of the sea.

Seraing

1

At an untrodden height such a beam
of sunlight shines inside the factory
your fingers grip the fine dust the handrail

the beam between your legs above the depths
the twinkling from the heap of shards
springs up through iron latticework under your feet

onto the smooth face of the slate
falls as a beam of light through the window
the brown glow in your black hair.

2

Far above the debris on the floor
there's a shape imprinted in the dust
which had been wet then dried again

with a wood-grain pattern running
through it the lines crisscross your palm
grasping the handrail your curled fingers

the sunlight falls as a beam into the hall
sand in an empty industrial fan
the height ties a belt round your belly.

3

Dents and gouged slogans
in blocks of wood that drop to the ground
untrodden your fear of losing balance

the rubble lying there the remains of streets
rag sacks with earth piling out of them
the stripe through one of your eyebrows

a rock in your hand black with the dust
in an arc of light high in the factory hall
the steel steps the hem of your coat.

4

When at a height you've never known
a rainbow caught between your slightly parted legs
measures the window's diameter its circumference

holes in metal the grass in the guttering
your feet side by side on latticed steel
a tangle of struts amongst the stone

your fingers draw stripes trace lines
out of the factory through the gap in the fence
along the railway track toward the river.

5

From a dizzying height the roofs and zebra crossings
balls that weigh down the power lines
holes in corrugated iron swing windows left open

the light in the display in front of the net curtains
sofas in the street children jostle by the gate
their fingers in the fencing and the bottle

upside-down over your cupped hand water
with coal-dust dissolving in it a pool
under the door which reflects what's inside.

6

Wind steps in and leaves
a lingering echo a drop falls a patch
of damp gleams in the dust every sound

seems human the clink of stone
on stone a ladder lying level the heap of pallets
you're sitting on and the voices that are not there

a tinny church-bell the noise of cars
the clank of a train the leaves on the
steps the puddle of shattered windscreen.

7

Smoke seems to well up so deep beneath you
that your eyes force the shadows back where
they belong the dust rises from the ground

your hand grasps the rail beside the stairway
blue lilacs grow out of the gravel
steel sheets curl in the corners

chunks of concrete on their side reinforced with wire
the holes in the metal landing the cracks
between them your soles over powder that wafts away.

8

Reef-knots in a torn-off piece of rope
hanging from the rail of the gantry your leg
skids through the iron into the grating you buckle

slump and take refuge on a landing where
you roll down your tights staunch the bleeding wipe
away the dirt with a cloth the handrail twisted inwards

the heap of glistening slates the fallen meshwork
the drumming on the corrugated panels
the collapsed caterpillar tracks and open dumpsters.

9

You drop your hand there's nothing you dare
to lean on nowhere to hold onto the coil
of thin metal strips around you the missing rung

the wheeling shadows wind tugs
at the roof sets it clattering bangs
the corrugated iron against the cross-stays

the footstep planted deep in the powder
it's getting dark it will soon be night
but everything stays silent and gray under the dust.

10

Sunlight comes from under the corrugated panels
ocher like coals burning behind glass you spread your
fingers draw black stripes across your belly

the wound stings the beam rips frayed sacks
open the torn scraps of rope the light falls
into the open maw of one of the diggers

clouds gnawed at the edges by the sun
the teddy bear on one buttock beside the stairway
smoke from the thick pipes against the horizon.

Man in the Water

An armless woman is standing by the lake
outside the spaceship disk of a teahouse
you imagine how she lifted up her arms
and tossed them flying into the sky
the woman looks at you open-mouthed
you stretch toward your two arms through the water
you lost your wedding ring in the rose garden
your wristwatch always runs an hour fast

on the fallen clump of trees across the water
you see birds' nests and black beetles
a duck swims slowly towards you
turns its beak and you see its eye
in which the lake is round and blue
your legs float across the pond's soft shallows
over ooze and wisps of mud
the water is cold your coat swells out
and undulates along the ripples of your fall
the duck quacks and veers away from you
tree branches rock along the waterline

day is breaking the light is rising
when the woman stoops to the water
drinks the lake dry with her open mouth
you're lying in a hollow your hands in the mud
you lift your chest and slowly stretch
you pull your hands from the sludge with a plop

and place them just above her armpits
where her arms used to be
her hair is short her breasts are small
the stone feels warm her neck unblemished

and you feel her power to lift you up
her will to pull you out of the earth
and throw you high into the sky
toward the clouds the sun the planets
the milky way the dust of stars
right through the vowels of your name
erasing the roundabout ways you took
before the summer you arrived on earth
a wind blew up that didn't last long
and the blossom landed between the wheat.

Rowers on Lake Aa

1

Jetties in the middle of the lake
race numbers and balloons

ridges across the water

arms crossed a rower
holds the blades still on the water
then leans back and pulls on the oars
and bends forward and pushes them up

the quiet squeak of the oars through the rowlocks
the slapping of the water

plants dangling into the water
floating along with the current

patter of wings on the lake
croaking of frogs in the park.

2

What do you think of while walking the street?
what I think of

a tree standing there, holding its load up high

the way a frog croaks: first a squelchy whinging
then a jokey tick-tock cackling

the streetlights on the other shore
a rower through the dusk

water which gives the quayside back its view

water which is invisible in the dark
silence, since there's no land, just water.

3

Like a cloth folding in two a heron takes flight
spreads its wings and hangs in the air

wavelets till the end of the lake

the yelling of the cox
the grunting of the rowers

the echo from the speakers

a helicopter vanishes behind the trees
a dog slurps loudly from a bowl

flashing lights of a flatbed truck
neon sign on the corner of an apartment block
stacks of bucket chairs in the grass.

4

Water I need to see
so I can lose myself

jagging of contours
the borderline between ripples and stillness

white clouds on the water
rings expanding across the waves

the muscles under the skin
the palms that grip the raw wood

the crease across the waterline
tire tracks through the grass.

5

What's the tune that I keep singing
whose song I can't recall?

synchronised blade-strokes on the water
a coot beating its wings as it lands

trees that dangle over the banks
and hide the waterside

orange trashcans lined up in the grass

the light in the middle of the lake, the quivering leaves
the undulating surface

water heading nowhere in particular.

6

Coolness on the arms
on both cheeks, in the back of the neck

water that reflects my sight

the painter tricking us
with what he sees in the water

blue-gray skies
trembling surface waves
the far side near, the lake a canal

a boat turns
across the width of the water

shower of drops as fish spring above the waterline
a mossy tree-stump sways

the creak of the jetty
the quack of a duck

mist in cotton wisps on the grass
through the woods the sirens of the fairground.

7

Motor mower standing by the lake
concrete spheres across the grass

fishing line twisting across the water

rowers in the distance
hollow echoes on the lake

trees are shivered into wavelets on the water
a duck swims over a drifting nylon line

buoys in the middle on each one a gull

water a mirror which tells me
I want to be inflected.

8

Ducks bathe in flooded grass

a square tower between the trees
a spire juts above it

water seems viscous in the twilight
and drifts past me like an oil-spill
the dark woods in duplicate

water hemming the jetty green
orange light under the bridge shading the lake red
ripples wiping away the gleam

the footpath under water
sounds from the city across the bathtub of the lake.

9

The stripe of light on the path
out of the woods, into the day

the water I need
so I can lose myself

rowing boats upended
sixteen oars on the path
ducks jostle in the grass

joggers in the darkness

the gray of the clouds
and the gray of the water
and the gray of the rain in between

the wind rises
when the storm has passed.

10

Streetlight is lost in the reflection of the sun
birds twitter on the bank

a woman pushes up her black woollen sweater
and scratches her belly
a man in a wetsuit dismantles a jetty

a dog on a long lead
a woman with a heart on her T-shirt

a man, a woman—eight rowers groaning

lamps in the rose-bed which slowly
leach the light out of the air
as water washes the excess out of me

the loudspeaker under the bridge

the cord low over the watercourse.

~

Light-lines on the horizon pull the sea into the sky
light-lines in the sea

the sun lies in the bowl of the clouds
which take away its shape

horses walk in file along the sand
poles down the beach and into the sea, each topped with a bird

a ship in the white of its foam
brightness stippling my eyelid

cargo ships pushing the water out of their way

sandbanks in the bay
waves washing past them onto the shore

crickets in the marram grass
footprints whose heels crack open the hard crust of sand

sand with just a few shells
patches melding together across the sea.

~

Alarmed by a constant throbbing across the soundscape
the teeming of the pebbles in the floor

the line of trees evenly spaced along the canal

light slanting sharp onto the eyes
at the moment you arrive

grass ascending the slope
stripes straight up the dike

where you throw the sand back into the sea
in your eyesight the boat
is the highest point on land

land vanishing in a swirl where the sea turns a corner

the mouth opens like a golden cage
the mist above the field the ditch like a mirror.

~

The wind pushes you back onto the island
sand plumes up from the dune

a greyhound scatters the seagulls
as it runs through the shallow stretch of sea

grass rippling across the dip in the dunes

the tangle of driftwood, chunks of concrete in the sand
the frenzied fluttering foam

How can the eye have swum away?
In what? To where?

stretched out by the horizon
your long shadow across the breadth of the beach

rain taps against your skull
crows flitting from the lock-gates to the ferry.

~

Everything hangs dead level, the waning
moon
the date on the wall

she's at the table putting out the silence
he's rinsing the windows dark

shards from the hours we sit together
shipless in the dark rain

the pigeons which suddenly all take flight
the eyes on the branches in the square.

Translating poetry, for me, involves three processes layered over each other. In the first, surface layer, I work out the word-meanings, images and poetic forms that the "source" (original) poem uses. I write my findings out as an English literal poem-plan, with lots of alternative wordings plus notes and queries. In a second, underlying layer, which happens both during and after the first, I look beneath the source poem's surface. I tease out allusions and unwritten assumptions, and explore why the poet wrote what they did. These insights are added to the poem plan. I then use the plan to write a first draft of the translated poem. My aim as a translator, by the way, is to recreate the source poem's imagery and poetic drive in an English-language poem—so to give neither my own poetic riff on the source, nor a literal crib. Though this aim already drives my first draft, it takes many redrafts till I feel I've achieved it.

In these first two processes, collaborating with others is essential. With this collection, I checked I had understood the source poems correctly by running each first draft plus my queries past Erik Lindner (who has excellent English) and my wife Hanneke Jones-Teuben (who is a full Dutch-English bi-lingual). To-and-fro emails between Lindner and me helped firm up the second, subtext layer—the references to Walter Benjamin in "18 September 1994," for example.

The third, deepest-level process happens more slowly, and unconsciously. It involves absorbing the poet's vision and voice, and developing an English counterpart. This counterpart, I feel, is what the poet might have used if they were writing in English. But it should still convey the refreshing force of the new, which the poet brings because they are writing in another poetic tradition. What makes Erik Lindner's poetry special for me, in fact, is his vision and voice. One aspect of this is his almost filmic way of seeing and telling. "Witnesses at the Threshold 1," for example, builds a Dutch semi-rural landscape with a sequence of close-up shots: windmill-sails and birds, dogs by houseboats on a canal, and so on. In my final English version:

Birds tilt at windmills
all in a whirl

barking by the houseboats
chains drag through the gravel

cartwheeling like clockwork
high in the sky

[…]

the gallery round the tower
its guardrail slanting outward

a river flowing
into a marshy field.

Linder's poetic camera, moreover, records without commenting—this, to my mind, gives his poetry its compelling strangeness. In Dutch, he uses verbal nouns and relative clauses to give a sense of actions as film-shots: "een regelmatige radslag" (literally, "a regular wheel-turn/cartwheel") and "een rivier die uitmondt" ("a river which debouches") in the above lines, say. In English, I now see that I typically convey this with -*ing* nouns and adjectives: these two images became "cartwheeling like clockwork" and "a river flowing," for instance.

A second aspect of Linder's vision is his poems' settings: often Dutch landscapes, interiors and, especially, coastscapes. These can often be recreated in English by translating literally. Or with slight tweaks—changing "molen" ("mill") to "windmill," for instance. Sometimes, however, non-Dutch readers may not have the knowledge to visualise the wider setting behind Lindner's zoomed-in images. In "Witnesses at the Threshold 1," say, Dutch readers would know that "de overhellende balustrade / aan de rand van het plateau" ("the leaning balustrade / on the edge of the round platform") is part of the windmill mentioned earlier. Most English-language readers, however, are less familiar with Dutch windmill architecture, so I gave them a clearer steer: "the gallery round the tower / its guardrail slanting outward."

Occasionally, I also added such missing knowledge in endnotes: mentioning that the Leiden Lakenhal (in "Tokens of Identity 1") is a museum, for instance. But end-note information should always be an optional add-on, I feel. You shouldn't need it to read the poem. Moreover, over-interpreting—whether in poems or endnotes—risks diluting the voice of the poet with that of the translator as pedagogue. After discussion, Erik Lindner and I decided, for instance, not to add a note telling that *Acedia* was inspired by the Flemish landscape where World War I was fought. We felt this would have robbed the poem of its open-endedness by implying it was simply about one event.

Linguistically, Dutch and English are close cousins. This doesn't mean that the surface, text level of translating Linder's poems was always easy. In *This forme fits somewhere*, for instance, none of my Dutch-English dictionaries (one paper tome and three on-line freebies) nor my big Dutch-Dutch dictionary contained the word "zetvorm." Googling it, my usual backup strategy, gave a couple of Dutch texts referring to something like "layout," which didn't fit the context. Luckily, strategy number three—asking the poet—paid off. Lindner explained it was a metal frame to hold a page of lead type. After that, half an hour's researching English-language websites about printing gave the word "forme."

Again at text level, Lindner sometimes also uses idiom-play—deploying an idiom in both its literal and in its figurative sense. In Dutch, line 1 of "Witnesses at the Threshold 1" is "Klap van de molen" ("A blow from the mill"), for instance. Idiomatically, this means 'something that sends you crazy,' like being hit by a whirling windmill-sail. But line 2, "vogels in de wieken" ("birds in the mill-sails"), shows that the mill is also a real one. Here, the problem is that idioms are often culture-specific. Hence Dutch, unsurprisingly, has more idioms about windmills than English. My normal go-to expert, a 1940s doorstopper of a proverbs dictionary, suggested "tilt at windmills" as the only English idiom linking mills with craziness. When I ran this past Lindner, he mentioned that "Klap van de molen" could also mean that the sails stop moving "in één klap" ("in one blow," i.e. suddenly), so that birds can perch in them. This was an idiom too far: I couldn't work this into the stanza. Instead, I brought the birds into line 1, and in line 2 added another image linking mill-sails with craziness: "Birds tilt at windmills / all in a whirl." Which Lindner felt was fine.

This translation challenge and solution show two things. Firstly, Lindner is the translator's ideal source poet. He answered quickly and in detail all my nit-picking questions. and alerted me to any misunderstandings in my drafts. But no less importantly, he gave me the freedom to decide what final renderings sounded best to my native-English ear.

Secondly, poetry translation often involves re-*creating*, not simply reproducing. Over three centuries ago, John Dryden described poetry translators (at least those who, like me, try to be both faithful and poetic) as "dancing on ropes with fettered legs." Poetic fetters, however, are not always harmful. Michael Holman and Jean Boase-Beier, for instance, argue that constraints stimulate the translator's creativity. I feel, in fact, that creativity—as long as it is guided by the faithfulness to the source poem's imagery and poetic drive—is what enables translators to do the source poem justice. As I hope I have done throughout this book.

Francis R. Jones

NOTES

18 September 1994: The poem relates to a visit to Portbou in Catalonia, where Walter Benjamin died in 1940, and where a memorial to him now stands.

Ourcq: A Northern French canal.

Tokens of Identity: In Renaissance times, rhetoric societies ("rederijkerkamers") played a key role in Low-Countries literary life, arranging recitations, poetry competitions, etc. A painting by Cornelis Cornelisz van Haarlem in Leiden's Lakenhal (Cloth Hall) museum portrays a local society's member in his role as jester.

Duindorp is a white working-class neighbourhood by the North Sea in the conurbation of The Hague.

The Tramontane: Here Lindner references his visit to Portbou (see note to "18 September 1994"), pictures of corals and a cliff-face by Dutch poet/artist Rik Lina, and a near-fatal diving trip by Lina off Portbou. The tramontane (a fierce north wind) was blowing, and there were unexploded wartime bombs on the seabed. When the group leader entered an underwater cave, Lina and his companion lost him. Running out of oxygen, the pair resurfaced, could not find their boat, and were swept away by the current—but this brought them to the boat, with the group leader already in it.

Ostende: The French spelling of the title alludes to Henri Storck's silent film *Images d'Ostende* (1929) about the Belgian seaport and resort of Ostend.

Klockmann: The title refers to the art jeweler Beate Klockmann.

Ivens and the Wind: The poem was inspired by the 1988 film *Une histoire de vent (A Tale of Wind)* by veteran Dutch director Joris Ivens.

Witnesses at the Threshold: Poem 4 alludes to Jan van Eyck's painting *The Arnolfini Wedding* (1434).

Wake: The cycle was created during a residency in Ostend for Flanders & Netherlands Guest of Honour, Frankfurt Book Fair 2016.

Seraing: Seraing is a rust-belt town in Southern Belgium. This poem was inspired by several visits to a derelict factory now used as a store and dump for municipal constructors.

Man in the Water: At the "Lonely Funeral" ceremonies in Amsterdam, held for those who die without friends or relatives, a poet reads a specially-written poem. This poem commemorates a Lithuanian man who drowned in the lake by the Blue Teahouse in the Vondelpark.

Rowers on Lake Aa: Lake Aa (Der Aasee) lies close to the centre of Münster in Germany.

"Alarmed by a constant throbbing across the soundscape": "the mouth opens like a golden cage" is quoted from Dutch poet H.C. ten Berge.

"The wind pushes you back onto the island": "How can the eye have swum away? / In what? To where?" is quoted from Paul Celan ("Wie kann das Auge fortgeschwommen sein? / Worin? Wohin?").

ACKNOWLEDGMENTS

The original Dutch poems first appeared in the following collections by Erik Lindner:

"Words are the Worst," "18 September 1994," "Island" and "Reason": in *Tramontane* (Amsterdam: Perdu, 1996).

"Ourcq," "If I'm lost for words," and "Tokens of Identity": in *Tong en Trede* (*Tongue and Step*, Amsterdam: De Bezige Bij, 2000).

"There's blood in your lips," "To Acedia," "The Tramontane," "In Zeeland," "Ostende," "The garden lies between the road and the window," "A man is eating an apple in the park," and "Back from Acedia": in *Tafel* (*Table*, De Bezige Bij, 2004).

"The sea is purple at Piraeus," "Klockmann," "A short woman holds an umbrella high above her head," "In the storm that just blew up," "This forme fits somewhere," and "When I walk toward the sea": in *Terrein* (*Terrain*, De Bezige Bij, 2010).

"Ivens and the Wind," "I remember," "Witnesses at the Threshold," and "Acedia": in *Acedia* (De Bezige Bij, 2014).

"Wake," "Seraing," "Man in the Water," "Rowers on Lake Aa": in *Zog* (*Wake*, Amsterdam: Van Oorschot, 2018).

"Light-lines on the horizon pull the sea into the sky," "Alarmed by a constant throbbing across the soundscape," "The wind pushes you back onto the island" and "Everything hangs dead level, the waning" have not yet been published in book form.

Earlier versions of poems in Francis R. Jones's English translation appeared as follows:

"Witnesses at the Threshold": as a chapbook, Jan van Eyck Academie (Maastricht, 2015); in *The Wolf* 33, 100-103 (2016); and online in *Enchanting Verses Literary Review* XXVI, 100-103 (2017).

"To Acedia," "Back from Acedia," "The sea is purple at Piraeus," "A stairway leads into the sea," "Reason," "If I'm lost for words," "The garden is between the road and the window," and "A man is eating an apple in the park": online at *Poetry International Archives / The Netherlands / Erik Lindner* (2016).

"Rowers on Lake Aa" (Parts 1-6, 8-10): online at *citybooks / Münster / Erik Lindner* (2016).

"Man in the Water": online at *Poetry at Sangam* (2017). "18 September 1994": as subtitles to Winfried Bettmer's film *Port Bou* (2018).

With kind thanks to the original publishers.

We would also like to thank Hanneke Jones-Teuben for her close reading and comments on the translations, and Victor Schiferli of the Dutch Foundation for Literature for his support for this project.

Stephen Scobie • Peter Dale Scott • Deena Kara Shaffer
Carmine Starnino • Andrew Steinmetz • David Solway
Ricardo Sternberg • Shannon Stewart
Philip Stratford, trans. • Matthew Sweeney
Harry Thurston • Rhea Tregebov • Peter Van Toorn
Patrick Warner • Derek Webster • Anne Wilkinson
Donald Winkler, trans. • Shoshanna Wingate
Christopher Wiseman • Catriona Wright
Terence Young